I Wonder If I'll See A Whale

For Katy,
the first Weller a-questing
on Stellwagen Bank;
and for our favorite, Trunk,
the first humpback found singing in the Gulf of Maine
—FWW

To our giant brethren in the sea
—TL

FRANCES WARD WELLER

I Wonder If I'll See A Whale

illustrations by TED LEWIN

The Putnam & Grosset Group

I wonder if I'll see a whale. We've left the wharfs of town behind, plowed past the lighthouse on the point. Now our fat, sturdy boat rocks, quiet, on the water. Watchful, waiting.

I hug the rail and hope. This morning, will I see a whale?

I've come before, in morning fog and when a sunset turned the sea all pink, and whales were here. But what I saw were spouts far off and shadows in the mist. It was a mystery, like Hide-and-Seek or Blind Man's Bluff, a game of chasing giants who would not be caught. I wouldn't say I've really seen a whale.

All around us, swells that stretch on to the sky seem empty. But down one
hundred feet a sunless garden lies. It feeds the clouds of fish that lure the whales.
The humpbacks come in spring from warmer waters—from winters filled
with songs of courting and the birth of baby whales. The crews who ride these
boats have named them for the shapes of fins and markings on their flukes.

There's Appaloosa, tail all speckled like a pony's back. Trunk, with a stubby dorsal fin. And Midnight, with a tail all black. Stormy, on watch beside the wheelhouse, knows every one. "You keep watch too," he says. "You might spy something the lookouts miss."

And so I watch. I watch so hard and far my eyes play tricks. Each dash of spray could be a whale's spout. Each wave's trough seems to hide a creature's back. And when I blink I still see skipping light.

But where are Midnight, Trunk and Appaloosa now?

"A spout, to port!" a lookout calls. "Off to our left, a fin whale up to breathe." But Stormy says the humpbacks are the ones who come to boats. So as the engines rumble louder, I just sigh. Another speedy whale that won't be caught.

My jacket's hot. I tie it round my waist, just as a shout goes up beside the other rail. My heart does little jumps as if I'd found a hider's secret place. But it's a chain of dolphins rippling by, only playing. Not leading us to humpback whales.

The climbing sun grows hotter on my neck. I pull my sweater closer like a scarf and wonder if I'll ever see a whale.

"Two spouts!" a lookout hollers, "dead ahead!" I see them, fat and low, mushroomy blown-out breaths of air and water. It's humpbacks, Stormy says! But now they've sounded, diving deep.

We hustle toward the spouts full speed ahead, only to ride the waves again and wait. The engines stop. The lookouts turn this way and that. It is like Hide-and-Seek. I hardly breathe.

Until "To starboard!" someone calls, and on our right rise mushroom spouts, a big one and one smaller. Sudden and gentle, a mother whale and baby roll right toward us, swimming side by side. Then they give spouting sighs and dive deep, showing us their flukes. I'd name that baby Snowball, for the big white circle on its tail.

The engines hum as if the captain planned to follow, but it seems to me they've gone. At least I've seen some whales. Well, backs and tails.

I hug the rail again and watch the empty waves. But as I watch, the cold sea starts to boil, as close as my backyard is to my house! Now my heart pounds. I tug on Stormy's shirt.

"Look now, to port," he says, so calm. The engines hush. The bubble circle grows. Some feeding whales, he says, blow bubble clouds to herd small fish ahead as they rise from the deep.

The water rolls and gaping jaws rise round the bubbling circle. And Stormy says, "Three humpbacks here."

Each monster mouth is like a pot aboil with creatures trying to escape. And whoa! From nowhere, swarms of birds swoop down. Terns. Laughing gulls. They're fishing in the whales' mouths!

And yet before I see the whole whales underneath those mouths, they sink into the swells and disappear.

I take a big, deep breath. Well, even if they're gone, I've seen those mouths. And backs and tails.

But all at once behind us—"Off the stern!" Another huge black body shoots into the air, white belly shining as the backward splash throws spray up higher than my house. "It's Trunk, breaching!" the lookout cries. "I'm sure I saw his stunted fin."

Through drifts of spray, I peer this way and that. And nothing's there. Right now, down deep, does Trunk's tail pump to send him shooting up again?

Oh, yes! He's breaching! Once, twice more—as if to say, "Hey, look at me!"

And he's not finished, for before the spray is gone, his tail pokes from the water in a whale's salute.

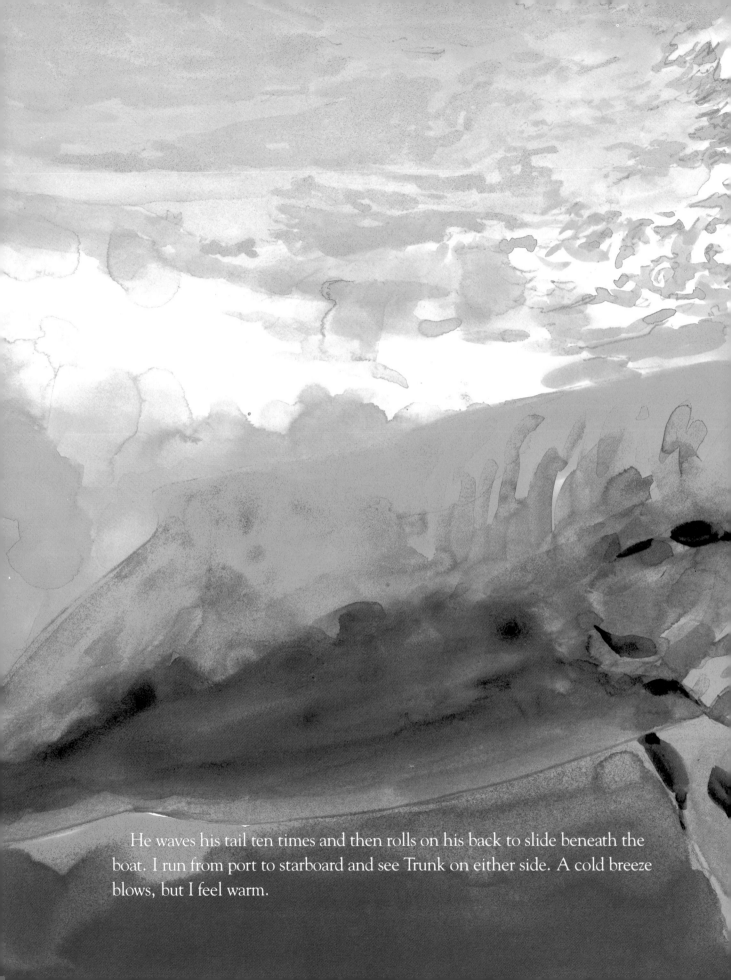

He waves his tail ten times and then rolls on his back to slide beneath the
boat. I run from port to starboard and see Trunk on either side. A cold breeze
blows, but I feel warm.

Now right in front of me Trunk's head comes up. "Ohhhhhh. There's a whale," I whisper to myself. And then there is a hush. I look at Trunk, and he at me.

It's not a game. It's more like church.

We're cousins, this huge whale and I—both mammals, breathing air and drinking mother's milk. And Stormy says man moved from sea to land, while whales gave up their legs and moved to sea. Maybe our great-great-great-great grandfathers were friends. Because he seems to know I've watched for him. Because he seems to know I've come in peace.

We have a good long look before Trunk starts to sink. His flippers are the last I see of him: white shadows in green water. The engines hum again. And Stormy says, "It's time we headed home." But what if Trunk's still here!

The boat swings round, but I stand by the rail and watch the wake. Right where we were, a huge dark head comes up, as if to say, "Where did you go?"

I lean far out and holler, "I'll be back!"

Trunk couldn't hear me. But I think he knows.

Whales migrate with the changing seasons much as birds do, and the same whales return faithfully to the same parts of the sea, such as the underwater banks off the northeastern coast of the United States. Whales roam all the oceans of the world, but thanks to cooperation between scientists and commercial whale-watching vessels, the whales in the Gulf of Maine are among the most thoroughly studied. Whale-watchers sailing from Province-town, Plymouth, Gloucester and other Massachusetts ports are likely to encounter both the enormous, fast-moving fin whale and the smaller, more playful humpback. Though all whales are threatened by persistent hunting and increasing pollution, rare Atlantic right whales and blue whales—both believed to be nearly extinct, gone forever—have appeared in these waters during recent summers.

Humpbacks, which average forty feet in length, have irregularly shaped dorsal fins and long white flippers that give them their scientific Latin name, *Megaptera novaeangliae* or "large winged New Englander." Known for their mushroom-shaped spouts and mysterious songs, humpbacks leap, lob-tail, slap their flippers and spyhop (raise their heads above the water, as Trunk does in this story), so that they seem to humans both curious and friendly. More than six hundred humpbacks have been identified as regular summer visitors to Stellwagen Bank, in Massachusetts Bay, and the Great South Channel, east of Nantucket Island. They spend the winter breeding season in the warm blue waters off Bermuda and the banks of the Caribbean.

Frances Ward Weller

I am indebted to Dr. Charles "Stormy" Mayo and his colleagues at the Provincetown Center for Coastal Studies, whose work inspired and informed this story, and to Dr. Robbins Barstow of the Cetacean Society International, who graciously provided information on whale-watching.

Special thanks to David Mattila, Irene Seipt and Karen Steuer of CCS for their patience in commenting on my manuscript and answering my questions, both reasonable and otherwise.

—FWW

Printed on recycled paper

A PaperStar Book, published in 1998 by The Putnam & Grosset Group, 200 Madison Avenue, New York, NY 10016.
PaperStar is a registered trademark of The Putnam Berkley Group, Inc.
The PaperStar logo is a trademark of The Putnam Berkley Group, Inc.
Originally published in 1991 by Philomel Books.
Book design by Christy Hale
Published simultaneously in Canada
Printed in the United States of America

Library of Congress Cataloging-in-Publication Data
Weller, Frances Ward. I wonder if I'll see a whale.
Summary: Aboard a whale-watching boat, a youngster observes the activities of a humpback whale. Includes factual information on the characteristics of whales spotted off the New England coast.
[1. Humpback whale—Fiction. 2. Whales—Fiction]
I. Lewin, Ted, ill. II. Title. PZ7.W454Iad 1991 [E] 87-10152
ISBN 0-698-11677-1
10 9 8 7 6 5 4 3 2 1